I LOVE MYTHOLOGY

Jason and the Golden Fleece

Text: Anastasia D. Makri
Illustration: Akis Melachris

Translated from Greek into English
Kiriaki Papakonstantinou
BA English Language & Literature / MA Psycholinguistics / DIPTRANS - DPSI
Chartered Linguist (Translator) / Translators - Interpreters Trainer
Member of the Chartered Institute of Linguists in London

UNDER THE AEGIS OF

United Nations
Educational, Scientific
& Cultural Organization

ΟΜΙΛΟΣ ΓΙΑ ΤΗΝ UNESCO ΝΟΜΟΥ ΠΕΙΡΑΙΩΣ & ΝΗΣΩΝ
CLUB FOR UNESCO OF THE DEPARTMENT OF PIRAEUS & ISLANDS
Πέτρου Ράλλη 210 & Θησέως 1 Νίκαια,
Τηλ: 210 4967757, Fax: 210 4944564 - www.unescopireas.gr e-mail: unescop@otenet.gr

AGYRA
publications

Η παρούσα έκδοση, Οκτώβριος 2014

Jason

Jason was the grandson of the first king of Iolcus, Kritheas. His father was Aeson and his mother the nymph Tyro. Jason was still an infant when his uncle, Pelias, usurped the throne from his father, Aeson. To protect Jason, his father sent him away to the mountains where he grew up under the care of the wise Chiron. Chiron was a centaur, half-man and half-horse. Chiron tutored Jason several things; among others to be honest and generous.

When Jason had come of age, Chiron revealed his true identity and which his origin was.

"It's time to go back home and claim what belongs to you", told him Chiron.

So, Jason set out to Iolcus determined to take the throne back. On his way he came across the Anavros River, on the bank of which a withered old woman was sitting.

"Will you help me across, lad" she pleaded. Warm-hearted Jason did not think twice. Taking the old woman on his back, he set off into the current. Yet, in his effort he lost one of his sandals. "Don't worry, lad, this is a good sign. I'll stand by you in everything you need", said the old woman, who was none other than goddess Hera in disguise, revealing herself to Jason on that far shore.

Both surprised and pleased by this meeting, Jason went on his way. A few days later, he arrived in Iolcus and went straight to the palace. On seeing him, his uncle Pelias was terrified. Gods had warned him that one day young man "who wears but a single sandal" would take his throne.

"I know why you are here, Jason. Yet, to give you my throne, you should first bring me the golden fleece", said

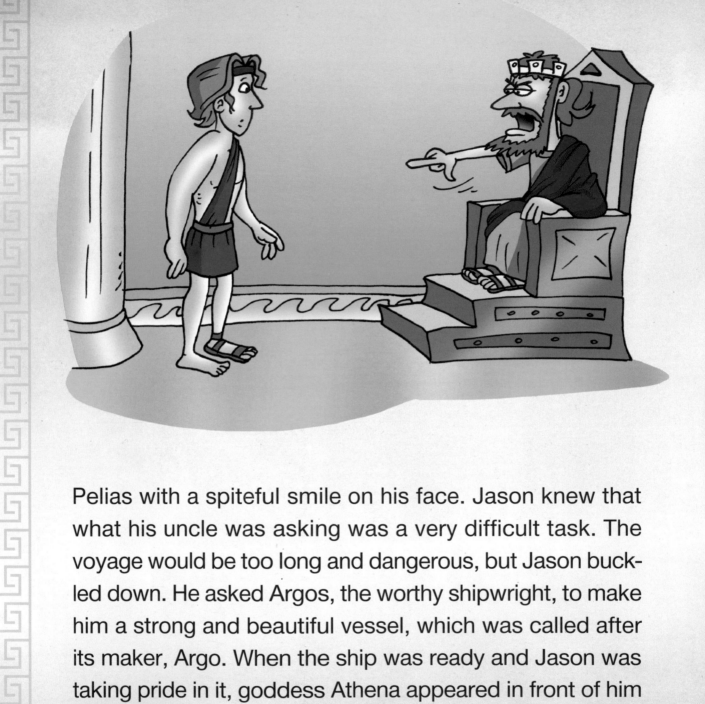

Pelias with a spiteful smile on his face. Jason knew that what his uncle was asking was a very difficult task. The voyage would be too long and dangerous, but Jason buckled down. He asked Argos, the worthy shipwright, to make him a strong and beautiful vessel, which was called after its maker, Argo. When the ship was ready and Jason was taking pride in it, goddess Athena appeared in front of him and gave him an oak branch as a talisman to protect his ship. Jason, all too happy, tied it on the bow of his ship.

4

When word went out throughout Greece about Jason's voyage, many heroes were ready to run the risk. Jason chose about fifty men. Among them were Orpheus, the greatest of all musicians, brave Hercules, Calais and Zetes, the winged twin sons of Boreas and Oreithyia, as well as Dioscuri, Castor and Pollux, the twin sons of Zeus. These were known as the Argonauts, after their ship. Thus, one morning they got supplies and set off in their ship. With the help of gods, tail winds helped the ship sail off.

The Adventure Begins

The Argonauts made their first stop at the island of Lemnos. There, something unprecedented happened – there were no men on the island. It seems that the women of Lemnos, for some reason, did not like men. However, goddess Aphrodite saw to the Argonauts were welcomed to the island. In fact, their hospitality was so warm that the travelers almost forgot the purpose of their voyage.

After the island of Lemnos, the voyage got really trying. They came across stormy seas and had to stop for supplies in places inimical, with hostile inhabitants. They had even to fight with wild beats; yet, they face all ordeals bravely and continued their voyage always tireless.

When they reached the land of bebryces, they met King Amycus. This savage king challenged all visitors to a boxing match and as he was so fearsome he always killed his opponent. So, once more he called out and the one who immediately accepted to fight was Pollux, the champion boxer, Castor's twin.

"Like hell you will win me! You seem rather to be tired of your life", said Amycus with an ironic laughter.

Pollux remained cool and as he was very agile and trained  he managed, after a long fight, to shatter him with a severe blow. Then Jason and the Argonauts flew to their ship to avoid the rage of bebryces.

The Harpies

The next stop of the Argonauts was a city in Thrace. There lived the blind seer Phineus who, punished by the gods, could not eat because his food was snapped by Harpies – monsters featuring the body of a bird and the head of a woman. The Argonauts wanted his advice on how to continue their voyage. Phineus told them: "I will help you, but first you have to save me from these horrible creatures that do not let me eat".

As soon as Phineus sat to eat, the Harpies rushed to snap his food. Then, Calais and Zetes, the twin sons of Boreas, fell on them with wings on their feet and swords in their hands. Soon, no Harpies were left.

Phineus thanked them for their help and told them that the greatest danger just ahead was the Symplegades or Clashing Rocks, two enormous rocks which clashed together upon any ship passing between them. So, he advised them what to do: "Have a dove with you. When you arrive there, let it go. If it flies between the rocks in safety, then you can do it too".

The Symplegades

Once the Argonauts arrived at the entrance to the Black Sea, where the Semplegades stood, Jason set the dove free. She managed to pass safely before the rocks clashed, only losing some feathers of her tail. As soon as the rocks rebounded Jason yelled: "Hurry up! To the oars! Let's pass now!"

However, there was head wind. Then, the goddess Athena sent a huge wave that pushed Argo; thus she suffered only a splintered stern.

Their journey continued peacefully until, before arriving in Colchis, they were attacked by the Stymphalian birds. Then the Argonauts started violently beating their poles on their shields. The clangor scared the dangerous birds away and thus the heroes were saved.

Shortly after that, they arrived in Colchis. They had a rest and the following morning Jason set off to meet King Aeetes. When he arrived at the palace, he was supposedly warmly welcomed by King Aeetes himself. Jason explained that he wanted the Golden Fleece to reclaim his throne from his uncle. "I'll give it to you", said Aeetes, "but first you'll have to yoke to the plough two fire-breathing bulls with brazen feet, and sow the teeth of the dragon".

Jason was listening to him carefully wondering how he could manage to perform all these tasks...

While Aeetes was speaking, his daughter Medea was standing by his side. The moment she saw Jason she fell in love with him and decided to help him.

Being a powerful sorceress, she made a magic potion and went to Jason in the middle of the night. On seeing her he was astonished. "Jason, smear your body with this magic potion and nothing can hurt you. On sowing the dragon teeth, giants will sprout. Then, throw a big stone among them and as they fight trying to find out who threw it, you will have the chance to kill them".

The next day, Jason gathered up all his courage and went to the field to anticipate the fire- breathing Bulls, who hit the ground with their bronze hooves. Everything around was burning but Medea's magic potion was protecting Jason. Thus, he managed to grasp the two bulls from the horns and have them harnessed. All spectators remained speechless. Then, Jason plowed the field and sowed the dragon teeth.

What happened then was something very strange and scary at the same time: immediately fully-armed fierce warriors sprang out.

Jason following Medea's advice took a very big stone and threw it among them. They started fighting accusing each other. Then Jason grasped the opportunity to kill them one by one.

The Argonauts were thrilled by such a victory; and so was Medea. Yet, the latter tried to hide her excitement, for fear her father suspected his daughter had helped Jason.

Then Jason went to Aeetes and asked the Golden Fleece. Unable to believe Jason's achievement, the king promised to give him the fleece the next day. Yet, other plans were in his mind; he was planning to send his soldiers burn the Argo and kill the Argonauts.

The next day, when Jason asked the Golden Fleece of Aeetes, he refused to give it to him. Jason and the Argonauts were enraged.

Then Medea, who knew her father's plans, met Jason secretly at night and told him he had to leave immediately, but before that she would help him get the Golden Fleece.

"But how will we pass the dragon who never sleeps but remains awake at the trunk of the tree?" asked Jason. "Don't worry about that. I'll take care of it", answered Medea.

Indeed, when they reached the huge oak they saw the horrifying dragon that looked like an enormous snake. On seeing them, the dragon started hissing, showing his teeth. Then, Medea approached him murmuring some strange spells, and sprinkled over him a sleeping potion which she had prepared. It was not too long before the dragon fell asleep. Then Jason climbed up the tree, seized the Golden Fleece and hastened with Medea to his ship.

"I got the golden fleece. Hurry up! Prepare the ship. We are sailing off!" Jason cried out to his companions.

While the Argonauts were preparing the ship, Medea ran to the palace to get with her little brother, the Apsyrtos.

Before dawn, Argo had already sailed well off the harbor. On hearing the news, Aeetes commanded his ships to chase them. They were about to reach the Argonauts when Medea had a horrible idea. She killed her brother and threw his body into the sea. When Aeetes saw Medea throwing her brother's lifeless body into the sea burst into weeping unable to believe his eyes. He immediately halted his ships and commanded his men to take Apsyrtos aboard. In all this turmoil, Argo managed to sail away. After what had happened, Aeetes could not find the courage to continue chasing the Argonauts...

Zeus, however, enraged by Apsyrtos' murder sent a terrible storm which found them in the Adriatic Sea and drove the Argonauts off course. Then Athena sent them a message that in order to be purified from sin of murder they had to visit the sorceress Circe, sister of King Aeetes and Medea's aunt. Indeed, once

they reached the island of Circe and met her, they explained the reason for their visit. Then Circe sacrificed a heifer to the gods and sprinkled Jason and Medea with its blood to wash away the sin. "The gods have forgiven you. You can go now", told Circe and they sailed back home after thanking her.

When they reached Iolkos, Jason immediately went to his uncle Pelias and showed him the Golden Fleece. Then he, unable to do otherwise, gave him the throne; thus. Jason eventually became a king.

Color the dot pieces to see
what the hidden picture is.

17

Connect the dots from 1 to 46
to see what threatens Jason.

Do all the necessary additions, subtractions, multiplications and divisions, retaining the original order of numbers, so that the result is number 9.

19

Put the letters in the correct order,
to see what hurt the dove's tail.

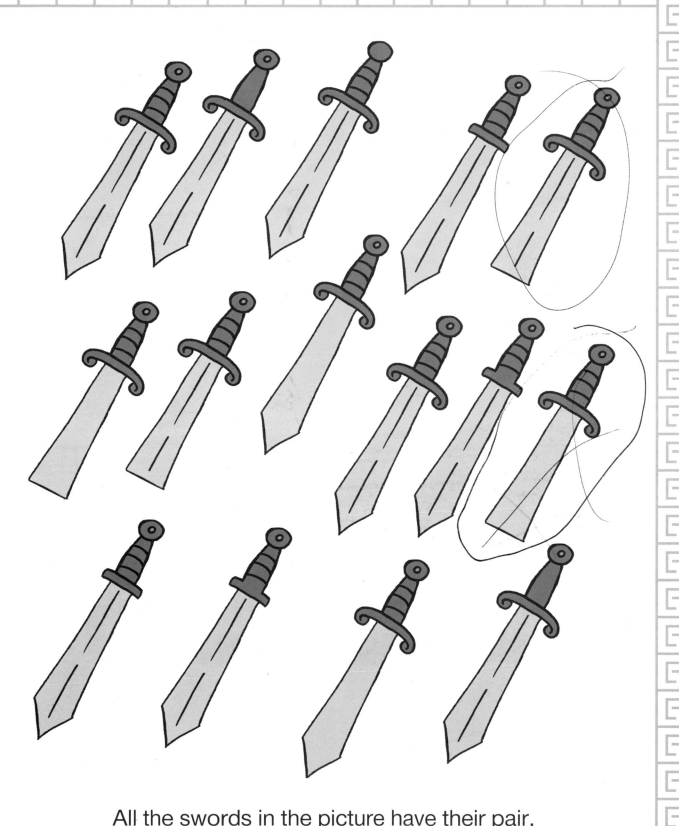

All the swords in the picture have their pair,
except one. Can you find it?

21

Can you find out which is the shadow of Medea?

Spot-the-Difference: Pictures 2 and 3 have 3 differences each
with Picture 1. Can you spot them?

Two out of the six details do not match
the picture above. Can you find which ones?

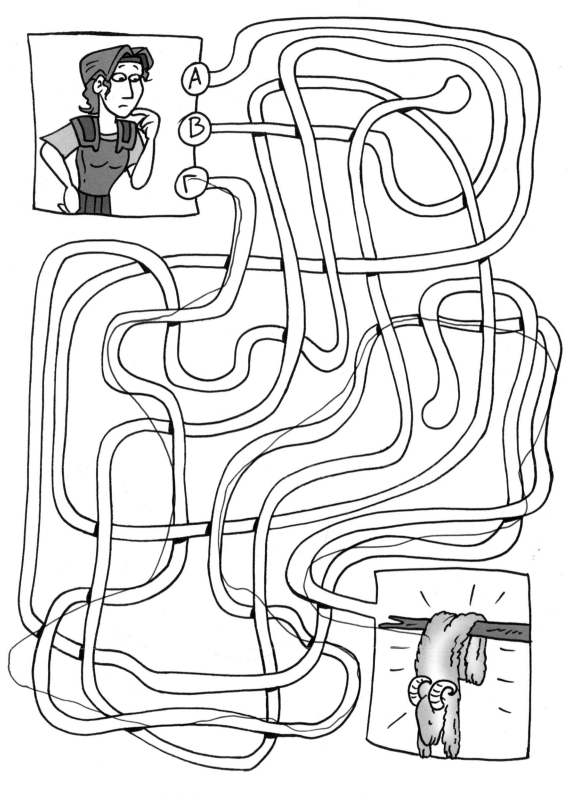

Which path should Jason take
to reach the Golden Fleece?

All the amphorae in the picture have their pair,
except one. Can you find it?

Which numbers correspond to the ship
with the white sail and the ship with the black sail,
so as to verify the operations?

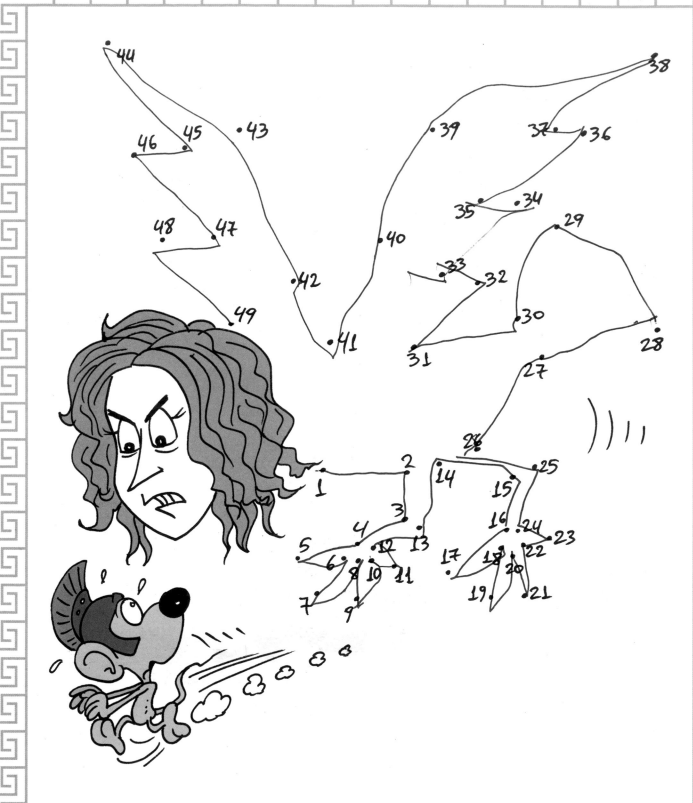

Connect the dots from 1 to 49
to see what scared the little mouse.

Spot-the-Difference: Can you find the 8 differences
between the picture and its negative?

29

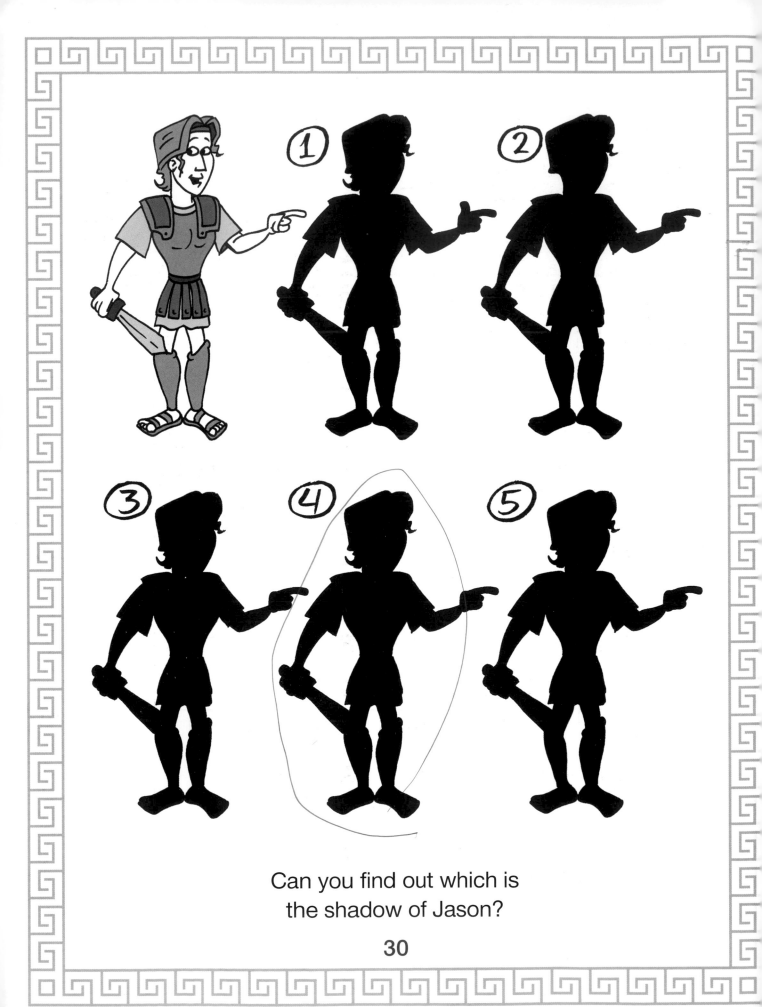

Can you find out which is
the shadow of Jason?

R	Y	N	T	Y	K	S	A	B	A	P	H	R	S
S	P	H	I	N	E	U	S	T	O	O	M	D	E
I	S	A	D	O	R	A	F	L	I	N	T	R	O
D	A	R	G	O	N	D	E	N	T	O	R	A	S
E	R	P	I	S	U	S	A	N	D	E	N	G	M
A	P	I	M	A	F	I	A	D	M	P	A	O	E
M	P	E	G	L	T	A	P	L	E	S	E	N	V
O	L	S	E	M	P	L	E	G	A	D	E	S	A
N	W	E	R	G	E	M	L	R	Y	R	T	T	R
E	H	A	Z	L	L	O	I	D	D	I	E	L	M
F	E	C	I	D	O	Y	A	I	S	L	S	E	A
E	C	Q	B	U	L	L	S	R	A	L	H	M	R

In the word-finding grid, horizontally and vertically,
there are 8 words relevant to the Argonauts campaign.
Can you find them?

SOLUTIONS

PAGE 17

PAGE 19 3+9:6x8-7=9.

PAGE 20 The dove's tail was hurt by the Semplegades (Clashing Rocks)

PAGE 21

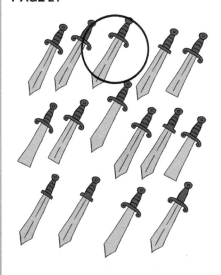

PAGE 22 Shadow No 2.

PAGE 23

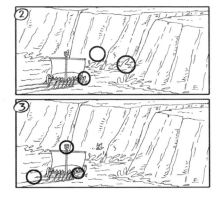

PAGE 24 Details No 4 and 6.

PAGE 25 Path C.

PAGE 26

PAGE 27 Black = 6, White = 4

PAGE 29

PAGE 30 Shadow No 4.

PAGE 31